AMERICAN

AMERICAN

"A Love Story"

Robert D. Padelford

authorHOUSE®

AuthorHouse™
1663 Liberty Drive
Bloomington, IN 47403
www.authorhouse.com
Phone: 1-800-839-8640

Published by AuthorHouse   10/09/2012

ISBN: 978-1-4772-7995-3 (sc)
ISBN: 978-1-4772-7996-0 (e)

Library of Congress Control Number: 2012919196

CONTENTS

INTRODUCTION AND ACKNOWLEDGEMENTS

He is around seventeen years old. He stands there in the bow of the ship as it rises and falls with the rhythm of the sea. Looking out over the horizon he can see the haze that is the promise of a new land. Occasionally he believes he catches a glimpse of a mountain top through the haze and thankfulness fills his soul.

This might be the story of a young man or woman today looking forward to a graduation ceremony and the promises that their future life holds for them. But it is not; it is rather the final chapter in the life of a young person on board the Mayflower as she completes her part in the journey to fulfill a destiny, the date is November 6, 1620.This is "a love story" called AMERICAN.

His journey has been harsh and during the voyage he has been overcome with a fever. Hesitantly he glances once more toward the promise and then feebly makes his way below deck to return to the cot where he has been confined for over a week. Laying there his breath becomes slow and shallow and in a final exhalation it ceases.

There is one man at the helm of the ship, one man on the mast, one infant in the arms of her mother and ninety nine men, women and children on their knees somberly acknowledging their absolute reliance on their Creator for the hope that is calling them.

His name is William Button, not significant is the archives of heroism, but undeniably etched in the book of eternity. He is a part of "a love story" that is American.

On April 18, 2012 at 6:30 in the evening I was privileged to be in an audience observing the induction of young men and women into the National Honor Society at Sunrise Mountain High School in Peoria, Arizona. Upon arriving there my thoughts were primarily on the completion of this manuscript and not particularly on the event that was taking place. As I sat down in the auditorium my mind quickly lost interest in its work and became focused on the music of the piano on the stage. I felt the brilliance of the pianist as the notes filled the auditorium, and my mind, with peace. As the ceremony progressed I watched these young men and women bring honor and respect to the inductees and to each other and to themselves. There was an air of caring and respect in the entire activity. I was elated by the dedication, devotion and love that I saw in the actions of the teachers and school officials. I thought "this same scene is being played out across this entire land", and I fell in love with my country once again.

Therein lays the hope that is tomorrow; love guides us still and fulfills our need to be a part of something greater than ourselves. To participate in the exercise of our passion, talent, spiritual gifts, with others, focused on the work before us, given completely to the task, being a part of a community of trusted friends. When mistakes are made to quickly acknowledge and correct them and to respond when help is needed, to consult with others or review the work when uncertainty occurs, without blame or fault finding, each individual continuing to strive for excellence in their performance and in that of the community they serve. This is American.

In writing this paper my desire is to bring a message of warning and of hope to the multitude of persons who will never be seen in the public eye, who without pretention, go about the completion of their daily responsibility. The only reward they are seeking is respect and love from within their community. The thoughts expressed here rightfully belong to some one else to whom I owe extreme gratitude. First of which is my Mom and Dad who guided me through my infancy into adulthood, teaching me to read, write, run and play. They taught the value in hard work and of individual responsibility. They instilled in me the love of family and the importance of integrity and honor in all of life. Because of them I know a personal relationship with the Creator and hold a deep respect for my country. I am in debt to the teaching community and the various clergy who brought knowledge, insight and motivation to me. My most sincere "thank you" must go to those men and women who have expressed great insight and knowledge in many of the texts and publications I have read, influencing my rationale. They are responsible for and must be given all credit for the thought and work that has gone into this writing.

Those thoughts and ideas herein expressed are compiled from a series of short writings that were penned over the last several years; insights inspired by experience, reflection and the expression of truths given to me from those other honorable persons.

To each of you, "thank you" and God bless you.

I

"AND GOD SAID"

A nd God said; Let us make man in our image, after our likeness:
and let them have dominion over the fish of the sea, and over
the fowl of the air, and over the cattle, and over all the earth, and
over every creeping thing that creepeth upon the earth.

The idea of being created in "our image" implies a physical sense
such as that between a father and his children while "after our
likeness" excludes or diminishes the thought of equality but still
maintains a personal relationship involving a general similarity of
our nature; of intellect, will, and authority. From the beginning a
door to a future relationship is established. There is no provision
for dominance by, or the deification of any authority other than
God. Each man is endowed with those same qualities, inclusive
in equal dominion, of intellect, will, and authority. From "the
beginning" our existence as individual persons held purpose
and meaning kept in the depth of God's love. Today that has
not changed. However, because of the self centered seeking of
personal ambitions this relationship has been forgotten. We have
replaced it with our own idea of the value and worthiness of
humanity. Self centered pride has separated us from truth.

Through history, even from Eve and Adam and their relationship with the temptation of self aggrandizement, and of the jealousy which possessed one of their children, this condition remains; a condition of the heart seen in the gift from Cain of the offering of a portion of his produce while his brother's gift was from the best of the best of his increase. Cain defined his action as equal in importance as that of Abels and in his jealous rage took his brothers life.

Even today, humanity is still seeking after a self defined importance—significance other than that for which they were created, such a position, if achieved, reaching its ultimate potential would bring absolute despotism. The strongest would prevail. The weaker would submit or die. One entity would remain holding the scepter.

Through time we have seen the effects of self seeking. We have witnessed, experienced and even been participants in tyranny, dictatorship, autocracy, authoritarianism, repression, absolutism; all of which are the result of a concentered self. The multitudes of people are held in hopelessness and fear, the will and intellect are suppressed, while authority remains under the dominion of the few

II

COMPASSION—THE MORAL SENTIMENT—PITY

'But when he saw the multitudes, he was moved with compassion on them, because they fainted, and were scattered abroad, as sheep having no shepherd,' MAT 9:36.

This word—*compassion*—as expressed in its original has a very special meaning; it expresses the deepest emotion of the soul. "It is to have the bowels yearn with inward affection; it is a yearning of the inmost nature with pity, or sympathy."

Even at the execution of the most vile criminal each one of us feels a sense of remorse and sadness in the ending of a life of a person created in the image of God. A person who has become so absorbed in self that it is now totally impossible for him to rationalize the existence of any authority other than his own. There is no force that will affect his reason. We see that person as totally depraved, even so, our sense of pity remains.

COMPASSION: THAT MORAL SENTIMENT OF PITY, OR SYMPATHY, A NATURAL CONDITION, INNATE IN MANKIND, BINDS US TOGETHER TO MAINTAIN CIVILITY. IT GIVES RISE TO THE SENSE OF JUSTICE AND IS BORN OUT OF OUR NEED FOR LIBERTY. IT ENCIRCLES FREEDOM, PLACING A LIMITATION ON MOTIVES OF SELF INTEREST AND GIVES BIRTH TO ALTRUISM.

PURSUED TO ITS FULLEST, PITY WOULD OVERCOME ALL EMNITY BETWEEN MEN; HOWEVER SUCH A PURSUIT WOULD BE IMPOSSIBLE BECAUSE OF THE FORCE—POWER—STRENGTH—OF SELF SEEKING; THE CHASM BETWEEN THE RICH AND THE POOR, BETWEEN THE EDUCATED AND THE ILLITERATE EVEN BETWEEN RACES, SEXES, NATIONALITIES AND RELIGIONS. EVERY (EACH) MAN, ENTRAPPED IN EGOCENTRICITY, ALSO HAS (SENSES) A NEED TO PITY WITHIN HIMSELF HENCE THE NEED FOR JUSTICE; A LONGING, PLEADING, AGONIZING NEED TO DO THAT WHICH IS RIGHT AND TO SET FORTH CERTAIN TERMS AND CONDITIONS WHEREBY EACH MAN CAN BE AT PEACE TO PURSUE LIFE WITHOUT HARM TO, OR FROM, HIS FELLOW MAN. THE RULE OF JUSTICE BRINGS FORGIVENESS, SETTING HIM FREE, OR MORE APPROPRIATELY, AT LIBERTY.

III

"IT IS CONSUMATED"

*** "Afterwards, Jesus knowing that all things were
now accomplished, that the scripture might be
fulfilled, said:" I thirst."
Now there was a vessel set there, full of vinegar. And
they, taking a sponge full of it, put it to his mouth,
therefor, when he had taken the vinegar, said: "It
is consummated" (Finished, or complete—made
perfect).

***The Holy Bible; Gospel of John; Chapter 19,
verse 28, 29, 30a.

Liberty was thus perfected at the cross. The requirement of
law was fulfilled. The law is no longer a curse but a blessing
and has become the guide to civility among persons, communities,
and nations. It has established rule and order, and given birth
to the awareness of man's unexhaustive need of forgiveness. A
birth fathered in the eyes of pity mothered in the eyes of love. It
is the greatest gift received and the greatest gift given. Through
forgiveness, whether in the offering of—or the receiving of, we are
no longer shackled nor imprisoned by our self imposed choices,
but free to pursue that for which we were created; to serve our
Creator in the redemption of humankind. He has appointed us to

bring the message of restoration to those who have not received it. This nation, The United States of Americans, was called into her existence to provide a safe haven where man could be at liberty to bring the message of His unfathomable love to this lost world. His law has established a portrait of justice reflected in the Constitution of our nation and has established order whereby we may pursue our appointed task. Each person having free will, intellect and authority can grow in a secure knowledge of the mission.

The document that forged the Constitution of our nation in its original was entitled "IN CONGRESS, July 4, 1776. THE UNANIMOUS DECLARATION of the thirteen united STATES OF AMERICA". Those representatives of the people of these states, there assembled in General Congress, made their appeal to the "Supreme Judge of the world for the rectitude of our intentions". Their appeal to the Creator was for their intention to be of righteousness—goodness, moral, correct, decent, of absolute integrity. "With a firm reliance on the protection "Of Divine Providence" they placed their signatures on that document, pledging "our lives, our fortunes, and our SACRED honor."

IV

PREDESTINED, OUR DIVINE CALL

The divine destiny of our nation was now established. Predestined to be the beacon of hope for all humanity, this nation expanded, bringing liberty to the lives of the people placed under her wing. Those thirteen original colonies were bounded on the north by Canada, the south by the Spanish Colonies, the east by the Atlantic Ocean and the west by the Mississippi River.—In time the territory of this nation under God has expanded. With the purchase of Louisiana from France (1803) and Florida (1819), Texas annexation (1845), title to the Oregon Territory (1846), the Mexican cession (1848), Gadsden Purchase (1853), Purchase of Alaska and the annexation of Hawaii, with a total of 3,718,694 square miles our territory expanded "from sea to shining sea". We are the work place where freedom and personal liberty are being served to people throughout the world. We are bound together by our will, our intellect, and our shared authority in order that we might bring His message of love to a lost world.—We have stumbled and fallen, even strayed away from our appointed destiny. He has always lifted us up out of our self induced oppression and placed us back on the road of our appointed task. We have expressed our penchant for self destruction, inflicting pain and sorrow on each other and on ourselves. Despite our attempts at self exultation His love has proven stronger and we remain that "shining city on the hill". We are not an instrument for dominion over any person or people but we are the light that leads them to the truth of our Creator. The lamp is still held high and is a beacon of hope to inspire those "humble masses"—not only here in our homeland, but to all people on earth.

THE NEW COLUSSES ***

Not like the brazen giant of Greek fame,
With conquering limbs astride from land to land;
Here at our sea-washed, sunset gates shall stand
A mighty woman with a torch, whose flame
Is the imprisoned lightning, and her name
Mother of Exiles. From her beacon-hand
Glows world-wide welcome; her mild eyes command
The air-bridged harbor that twin cities frame.
"Keep ancient lands, your storied pomp!" cries she
With silent lips. "Give me your tired, your poor,
Your huddled masses yearning to breathe free,
The wretched refuse of your teeming shore.
Send these, the homeless, tempest-tost to me,
I lift my lamp beside the golden door!

*** "The New Colossus"—Emma Lazarus—1883, the sonnet placed on a plaque inside the pedestal of the STATUE of LIBERTY

V

THE SOUL OF LEADERSHIP

FINDING THE SOUL OF A LEADER OR
OF A NATION

The soul, held captive by sin; enthralled, spellbound, enslaved, captivated, under the dominion of physical senses, tied to prejudices, habits, and social influences, controlled by circumstances, following impulses, seeking after an elusive happiness, incarcerated where there is no peace nor honor, no nobility nor resistance to wrong, driven onward by the fear of death,—finding itself without hope and utterly lost because of the lie of the senses and appetites, those excitable pleasures so intently pursued—weakly now, in a faint quivering voice cries out, "Oh GOD"

Does this speak of the soul of a victim of AIDS? Or perhaps of a man on death row? Maybe it is of a housewife who has been unfaithful or of a husband who has had an affair at the office? Or of a person breaking into their neighbors home? What about that of the C.E.O. of a multinational business—now bankrupt? A rapist? A murderer? A homosexual?

Could it be that it is of none of them, but perhaps of you?

Or even me?

How about the soul of this nation?

Perhaps it is the condition of man everywhere.

Perhaps this image qualifies a necessity for, or sufficiency in, the truth found in the condition of all men everywhere, having no defense, whose only plea is to weakly cry out "oh GOD,"

Perhaps it is the voice of those fainting, scattered, lost—having no shepherd, the multitude whom so much compassion was, and is still, being poured.

IN all the wandering and searching of our souls there has always been an awareness of a power greater than we could possess. In our total deprivation and absolute hopelessness our cry is heard and we hear His voice "Come back to Me, I am the Way"

PSALM of DAVID—103
Praise the LORD, O my soul;
all my inmost being, praise his holy name.
Praise the LORD, O my soul,
and forget not all his benefits—
who forgives all your sins
and heals all your diseases,
who redeems your life from the pit
and crowns you with love and compassion,
who satisfies your desires with good things

so that your youth is renewed like the eagle's.
The LORD works righteousness
and justice for all the oppressed.
He made known his ways to Moses,
his deeds to the people of Israel:
The LORD is compassionate and gracious,
slow to anger, abounding in love.
He will not always accuse,
nor will he harbor his anger forever;
he does not treat us as our sins deserve
or repay us according to our iniquities.
For as high as the heavens are above the earth,
so great is his love for those who fear him;
as far as the east is from the west,
so far has he removed our transgressions from us.
As a father has compassion on his children,
so the LORD has compassion on those who fear him;
for he knows how we are formed,
he remembers that we are dust.
The life of mortals is like grass,
he flourish like a flower of the field;
the wind blows over it and it is gone,
and its place remembers it no more.
But from everlasting to everlasting
the LORD's love is with those who fear him,
and his righteousness with their children's children—
with those who keep his covenant
and remember to obey his precepts.
The LORD has established his throne in heaven,
and his kingdom rules over all.
Praise the LORD, you his angels,
you mighty ones who do his bidding,
who obey his word.
Praise the LORD, all his heavenly hosts,
you his servants who do his will.
Praise the LORD, all his works
everywhere in his dominion.
Praise the LORD ,O my soul.

—in our moments of triumph and exuberance, of success and greatness, of winning and accomplishment this awareness in our soul still persists. It holds us in humility, keeps us from falling—it is our gateway to truth.

Where does all this fit into the soul of leadership, individually or in a nation?

Individually; confident of the call from our Creator, the soul longs to be of service, to be needed and to help others to fulfill their need. It must find a place where the abilities it possesses can find welcomed and needed expression, a right granted to us through the cross of Jesus. Our directive in leadership now is to bring the truth to all mankind, the message of His love for His creation.—to disciple and to be discipled—to follow and to lead. True leadership will seek out those attributes of persons and enable them to apply their peculiar gifts and talents to the task they have been given to complete.

This same principle, or responsibility, applies as well to our nation. Great followers make great leaders. Leading or leadership implies authority and, greater still, responsibility. Great leadership requires the inclusion of other persons in the process and demands awareness and respect for those attributes of authority, will, and intellect that are common to each of them. It further demands the understanding that the authority they have been given is a responsibility found in their service as being stewardship, to be maintained for a time and passed on to another.

Often alone, and in that loneliness, these three, leadership, authority, responsibility remain constant and are subservient to God alone, keeping His covenants, obedient to His precepts. They often arise out of tragedy, need, or despair and are in constant need of Prayer. Their work is to overcome the affects of pity or terror, always looking to the Truth in God's purpose for all humankind, seeking out others who, in time, are destined to carry on the work.

President Eisenhower, upon signing into law the addition of the phrase "under God" to our Pledge of Allegiance made the following observation—

> "In this way we are reaffirming the transcendence of religious faith in America's heritage and future; in this way we shall constantly strengthen those spiritual weapons which forever will be our country's most powerful resource, in peace or in war."

Destined? Under God, "those spiritual weapons which will forever", Ike was a man of God's choosing, he completed his appointed task and passed those reins of authority on to another. This is the roll of leadership, the high call of service.

Through time we have erected colossal monuments of remembrance to our great American leadership. Mount Rushmore portrays Jefferson, Roosevelt, Lincoln and Washington. Abe is again displayed as the "Lincoln Memorial". Near "ground zero" there is a form of a kneeling George and more recently we paid honor due to Martin King with the unveiling of the figure of a man stepping out of the stone—impressive, deserving, and bigger than life.

Perhaps, if we could ask each of them their opinion of these marvelous memorials of their service to mankind each one would say—"Thank you for your caring, however, I would personally have preferred a cross there, with my name at its foot."

There are countless others who could be named here who served the cause of the compassion of the cross, surrendering themselves to this mission that is American. Men and women who have worn this nations' military uniform, dedicating their lives to the purpose of liberty are to be named here.

VI

THE REVELATION FOR RESPONSIBILITY AND AUTHORITY

The authority, responsibility and need for leadership in our nation and in the Christian Church was evident in the event of 9-11-01. On 9-10-01; separation of the church from all societal affairs within our nation was prevalent.

The next day—"9/11"—an entire nation was joined together, singing "God Bless America" and praying for those who were suffering and in terror.

A revelation was given to the people of God. The "mantel of authority for the pulling down of strongholds" still lies upon the Christian church—going forward to "enlarge our territory, blessed of God, kept from evil, with His hand upon us" bold enough to say "Give me this mountain", trust sufficient to fulfill the authority that is ours.

A lost world is looking for this authority that is ours. As followers and servants of our Creator God and of our Christ and Savior there is no place for compromise or for complacency. For this nation to now walk away from our appointed task in the face of adversity is to deny our destiny and surrender our God given liberty; a gift from Him to each of our citizens and a gift we are to bring to all of humanity—which is our mission.

*** "For this blessed mission to the nations of the world, which are shut out from the life-giving light of truth, has America been chosen;"

*** (Excerpted from "The Great Nation of Futurity," John L. O'Sullivan, 1839)

Today the American is under attack from within. Men claiming to have knowledge but lacking wisdom are in positions of leadership. They were placed there by an injudicious electorate that has been deceived by their own complacency. However, there is now an undefined uneasiness stirring in our land. A people who have been mesmerized by dreams and promises of Utopia are awakening to the clamor of the lie imposed upon them as they slept. Still searching for an answer that will be found when they are willing to accept responsibility for their condition, admitting the transgression, renewing the covenant and relearning those precepts that created this nation of nations.

We must rediscover the purpose for which we were chosen; the mission to bring the message of that "life giving light of truth' to the nations of the world. This is the cry of the soul of our nation, to fulfill our destiny, to be American.

VII

THE REVOLUTION OF THE "LITTLE PEOPLE"

The following thought has been prompted by the "small people" comment from the Swede—Carl-Henric Svanberg, http://en.wikipedia.org/carl.henric_svanberg in his reference to the American citizens affected by the British Petroleum disaster on the coast of the Gulf of Mexico, and by a comment allegedly made by Leona Helmsley ("We don't pay taxes, only the little people pay taxes"), and also by a recently elected official in a campaign speech.

Down through the pages of history we have seen tyrants who destroyed freedom by denying people their livelihood and self realization, considering them to be no more than personal chattel—expendable at their will. Families of the biblical times suffered the same tyranny that the early colonies of our nation denounced and rejected. They knew the tyranny of painful taxation and the bitterness of prohibitive licensing that rendered impossible the opportunity of engaging in any form of legal endeavor unless delegated by the state. Individual ambition among the populous was held in contempt and even as criminal because intelligent thought was said to be "inborn" and therefore was not achievable by the "common" person. Therefore, persons were subjects of the king or state; their livelihood and their lives were totally dependent on those who ruled over them. However, the History of the United States reflects a refusal for any person to be denigrated to that condition, not for just a few, nor limited to those of this nation, but for all people on this earth.

Our nation has experienced its share of this tyranny. The loathfulness of those positions has given, and is still giving, rise to resistance resulting in their correction. Emancipation, Women's Suffrage, desegregation, etc. and yet today there still remains a progressive effort to re-affirm class distinction between our people, to reduces us once again to the former bondage of ignorance and repression, an effort to suppress truth, individual authority, and free will.

In the term "little people" lies a warning to the general populous, the "evinces" of "a design to reduce them under absolute Despotism".* This warning is to those of us who work each day, doing our jobs with integrity and purpose, paying our bills, meeting our responsibilities with honor, desiring peaceful rest at night, food and clothing for our families and believing that our elected leaders and civil authorities are actually in those roles of responsibility to preserve and protect our liberty—those "certain unalienable rights". We trust in their magnanimity and sense of justice, and through our lack of vigilance we have been betrayed.

Unlike many of the pundits and bobble heads in the media, I sort of like the term "little people". It has nothing to do with physical stature. There is something in the sound of it that is sweet and endearing. It calls to my mind "those humble masses" that are the vast majority of Americans, those of us who like singing about "The Star Spangled Banner". And those of us who believe "God Bless America" is a good thing. We share in the same cause, united in the same conviction as those who before us unanimously pledged to each other 'our lives, our fortunes, and our sacred honor."

We are the ones who are struggling today to honor our personal responsibilities. We are the ones who, underneath our own anxieties and concerns, care deeply about our neighbors, often more about their sufferings and hardships than our own.

We have remained silent while the news media, pundits, bobble heads, and our elected official representatives proceed to explain to us how bad things are because "somebody done somebody wrong" and they know how to fix it. Meanwhile they are attempting to pad their own wallets with the few dollars that we "little people" have remaining.

Personally, as one of the "little people" I am very weary of this: the lack of responsible leadership in this nation. Magnanimity has been replaced by self-seeking, blame is placed on someone else, very few are willing or even able to quickly address a problem, and if some one does attempt to intervene they are quickly viciously devowered by an evil media. Rhetoric is rampant while reason and logic are being ignored or even destroyed. And where is the work that is just and fair being done—action, the work that reveals character; the heart of a person and the heart of a nation?

Pray to the God of Creation that our leadership and each one our citizenry will be in-filled with, and regain, the heart of those who founded this nation, "for the rectitude of our intentions".

It is a curious thing that within the scope of that phrase "little people" lay a huge majority of persons who are there without the consideration of gender, race, education, ethnicity, age, religion, or political affiliation. Their commonality is found in the evinces of their citizenry in the United States of America. And there is no need for any other; not by the law that governs or by the will of our Creator; for it is by His will that we exist. We are a people united because of our individual right of freedom. The strength of our nation is dependent upon the personal liberty that is the right of each of her citizens. It is the responsibility of men and women who serve in leadership to guard and preserve that right for each person, individually. We are a race of people named American.

We are a people of law, a nation of persons who exist by our reliance on the protection of Devine Providence. Our governance is determined by the rules we have agreed to uphold, certain precepts derived from the commands of our Creator, brought to us through men who were inspired to solemnly declare and publish that each citizen of the United States of America is free and independent. In prayer and thankfulness, in study and thoughtful consideration, in wisdom and sober contemplation they established certain documents that continue today to maintain our individual right to be free, to life, liberty and to pursue personal ambition without injury to or from others. They also established a system whereby the mantel of those chosen to leadership would pass to others chosen by the electorate. We are American.

VIII

TRUTH—THE GREAT NATION OF FUTURITY

We are a nation born to lead, born in the mind of the Creator. A nation which, by His will, has been called to establish a base whereby men would be free to know, to understand, to apply and to teach the truth of His limitless love for mankind. Within our courts He established rules of governance for persons to live at liberty and to find and understand the truth. By His grace He has predestined certain men to fulfill HIS will; we have called them "hero" He has made them servants. This is a land existing under His wings where a person, free from all tyranny, can come to know His absolute truth and to be free to disperse that knowledge to people throughout the world. This is our call, This is AMERICAN. This is our "love story".

Mankind will hear the truth, and each one who hears shall accept or reject it by an act of their own personal will or choosing; this is being American; being free to follow after our own destiny to "establish on earth the moral dignity and salvation of man", immutable truth.

"Yes, we are the nation of progress, of individual freedom, of universal enfranchisement. Equality of rights is the cynosure of our union of States, the grand exemplar of the correlative equality of individuals; and while truth sheds its effulgence, we cannot retrograde, without dissolving the one and subverting the other. We must onward to the fulfillment of our mission—to the entire development of the principle of our organization—freedom of conscience, freedom of person, freedom of trade and business pursuits, universality of freedom and equality. This is our high destiny, and in nature's eternal, inevitable decree of cause and effect we must accomplish it. All this will be our future history, to establish on earth the moral dignity and salvation of man—the immutable truth and beneficence of God. For this blessed mission to the nations of the world, which are shut out from the life-giving light of truth, has America been chosen; and her high example shall smite unto death the tyranny of kings, hierarchs, and oligarchs, and carry the glad tidings of peace and good will where myriads now endure an existence scarcely more enviable than that of beasts of the field. Who, then, can doubt that our country is destined to be *the great nation* of futurity?" [*** Excerpted from "The Great Nation of Futurity," John L. O'Sullivan, 1839 *The United States Democratic Review*, Volume 6, Issue 23, pp. 426-430. The complete article can be found in *The Making of America Series* at Cornell University]

IX

THE BODY OF CHRIST IN WORLD LEADERSHIP

The following thoughts and opinions are not just my own but have been taken from various sources and from other writers with whom I agree and that I believe are proper and true.

"The condition of man <u>is</u> the affair of the Body of Christ, which is the Church. The world has no right to tell the Church how it is to think. It is not the role of humanity to determine the value of life."

The kingdom of God is ruled by our Sovereign Lord—every person is to be taught that it is the Creator God who has determined his or her worth, from the time of conception through eternity. All persons have a right to understand that truth. And it is the right and responsibility of the Church to disseminate that knowledge. Every person is to be informed of the value that has been placed on them by their Creator and all are to be invited into service in His kingdom. The authority for receiving or refusing that invitation remains within the will of each person.

The concept of leadership—whether it be in the political arena, or in the making disciples of Jesus, or in the community and in our personal lives—implies maturity; persons not only with the necessary knowledge, but who have demonstrated understanding, integrity, honor and wisdom and thru whom, by their actions Truth and Justice are made evident. Within the Church and within this nation men and women who exhibit these qualities have been called into certain positions of responsibility; all persons in leadership roles are to exhibit these same traits. All in leadership roles—elders, statesmen, trustees, senators, deacons, governors, representatives, presidents and disciples—are to be held to this same standard. However, the elder, as the name implies, has a greater accountability, for they are held to it. It is within the scope of the term "elder" where the responsibility of leadership in the dissemination of Truth is found.

Any given entity cannot, but rarely, rise above its leadership. No one person can run the affairs of a family, a business, a congregation, or a nation. This requires dispersion of responsibility, wise council and accountability. The character of persons in leadership cannot be over emphasized. Too often we are deceived by appearances and flattery or promises that appeal to our ego thus we refuse to consider the character of the person seeking our attention and approval. Conduct reveals character; in our election process we are recruiting people to a work. Bringing men and women into leadership—as being qualified to lead—is a slow and deliberate process. Placing them in roles, ether by election or appointment that they do not understand or for which they are not qualified is not beneficial to them or to the body in which they serve. It is better that a position remain unfilled than to give it over to incompetency or to someone intent upon the pursuit of personal gain or ambition. It is vital that each person receive and retain wise council.

To stress the need for diligence in this matter cannot be over done. American Civics needs to be introduced at the beginning the educational process and must be re-introduced into our current culture. A mature understanding of the meaning of "allegiance" and "republic"—"under God", "indivisible", of "liberty and justice", "one nation" is paramount.

- "The word is a discerner of the thoughts and intents of the heart".—*Heb. 4:12

The word—"The people perish for a lack of knowledge"—is as appropriate today as it was when it was first expressed. My sense is that it is even more applicable today, simply because it is on my watch. The knowledge that is required, or found lacking, is in the Holy Bible. The conclusion is that there is a great need of teaching from that source. Men and women of God must once again become the voice for which this nation was created.

The work, when completed, will always produce peace and joy; this is the gift from the Holy Spirit—all this is the duty of those of you who are in leadership, regardless of what the world is doing to you, saying about you or saying how you are to act. Remain steadfast in the role in which He has placed you. Your reward (our reward) is freedom and mercy and joy for all men everywhere as well as eternal life with our Creator. It is a gift we are compelled to share with those who have not received it; persons who are seeking purpose and identity in a lost world where there is no answer. This is American. This is American authority. This is American responsibility. This is American destiny.

Good followers make good leaders. Great followers make great leaders. This is true in the realm of eternity and it is also true in the realm of our nation. Leading or leadership implies authority and, greater still, responsibility.

X

TO COMPLETE OUR TASK,—
TO MAINTAIN SOVERIGNTY

As those chosen to leadership, placed in authority, given responsibility, what should we be doing?

*"If My people, who are called by My Name, will humble themselves and pray and seek My face and turn from their wicked ways, then will I hear from heaven and will forgive their sin and will heal their land." *2 Chronicles 7:1.

The Holy Spirit says it is time to root out those things that are unrighteous, refusing to tolerate unworthy thoughts, words, and deeds, and establishing virtue in every area of life around us as well as our own.

Our actions and conversations should—no,—must be gracious and attractive. Leaders must be on guard against all bitterness and malice, wrath and anger, clamor and swearing and insulting others. Those whom we serve should feel a sense of love, of joy and peace abiding in us as well as patience and understanding, kindness, goodness, faithfulness, gentleness and self control emitting from us.

Our battleground is where we are now established. Remain constantly on guard against selfish endeavor—within our own thoughts and actions as well as those with whom we are associated.

Our duty is to complete our appointed task. Hold fast to the ideal that has been placed in our care, exercising the peculiar gift each one of us has been given for its completion.

Our immediate purpose is to prepare others for service in the completion of our mission. Seek out others who can carry on the task when we are no longer able.

Our goal is for all humankind to spend eternity with the Creator.

This is American. Our mantel of protection is dependant upon our willingness to complete our task.

Within our nation we must maintain our God given sovereignty, adhere to those doctrines of freedom that have been bestowed upon us since our conception, and continually acknowledge our dependence upon our Creator, always seeking His guidance.

When those chosen for leadership fail in their mission civility decays and free men are no longer at peace. The unrest that prevails will, in time, demand new leadership if unity is to be maintained.

With the birth of our nation the rule of law was established to protect the civility and the person of each of her citizenry. That document has served our nation well for more than 200 years. It is the very core of our continuing existence and gives direction for the continuance of personal liberty for each of her citizens, providing a peaceful path on which leadership is to be transferred. Respect of law must be a priority for each one of us, and especially those of us who have been elected and appointed to leadership.

XI

THE COMMONALITY OF THE "LITTLE PEOPLE"

For a little while I am going to direct my thoughts toward those persons who are by reference, "the little people" (or the "small" people) of whom I am one. Recently ill-advised men have condemned my state for passing legislation that will protect you and me, legislation that would not have been necessary had our national leadership not failed us. The truly pathetic thing about their presence was they had no interest in reading or even understanding this legislation. Their primary goal was to focus attention on themselves, showing us how "important" they are and fattening their wallets. They promulgate racial bias and differentiate between classes of people to cause division and promote their personal wealth. Still other politicos, news media bobble heads and self-proclaimed experts, seeking worldly acclaim, joined in the fray with no consideration of truth, or respect for the rule of law. They believe that we are practically mindless and will accept anything they say as truth. That attitude prevails, not only in this one incident, but also in nearly all matters political and economic, an attitude, if allowed to prevail, will once again reduce us to absolute despotism.

There is something that has always bothered me and that I am going to express here. You might feel that it is not of great significance but my attitude toward it still persists and it happens whenever I hear the adjective preceding the proper noun, that being when the word "American" has a word that refers to a class of Americans preceding it, such as Irish American, or English American or for that matter Danish, Latin, African, Japanese, Chinese, Eskimo, Indian—I could list a few hundred more—I don't like it. I AM AMERICAN, WE ARE AMERICAN. There is no classification other than AMERICAN, we are one people. To claim any thing else is to deny our heritage. I am a member of the American race, not by the color of my skin or hair, but by my allegiance to this Republic, a nation under God, called by Him to suite His purpose, a nation indivisible,—the commonality of the "little people".

Something else that I know to be true; there are many of you who can do a far better service to your fellow Americans than our present elected leadership is doing. Consider that possibility for yourself and become active in the election process, even to becoming a candidate for election to an office. Look to other potential candidates who need your support. Find out what their position is on immigration and taxation, foreign policy, energy, oil, and natural gas, individual rights and responsibilities, abortion, religion, foreign policy, and listen to your own beliefs and ideas. Don't be swayed by opinions of the self exalted experts but listen to your own heart. Look to many different sources for information and knowledge, examine it and accept only that which you believe to be true. Prepare yourself to be at the voting booth at election time. If you find you can't personally become involved as a candidate, find the new guy who will, discover what his ideas are and support him if you believe he is right.

Our vote is the best way to get this nation back on the right track. We must go to the poles and express our convictions, not those of the leadership who are now in charge. Know and understand the difference. If freedom and independence are to thrive it is an absolute that every citizen must know what is truth and it is their personal right and responsibility to seek and to receive it.

[If you are as fed up over this constant barrage of quarrels, bickering, half truths and even out and out lies as I am—please—join me at the voting booth, To remain unmoved is to accept our bondage and to pass it on, as acceptable, to our posterity.]

In our history at one time the term "liberal democracy" was synonymous with "constitutional democracy". Today liberal democracy is non-existent. It is leading to a condition of despotism where governmental centralization, ethnic divisiveness, the erosion of freedom of press and religion, and unparalleled conflict within the citizenry is now present. Even more evident is the limiting of the citizenries authority of self determination and the centralized belief that government holds the mandate to do what ever it feels is best without the consent of the "uninformed" governed. The term "Progressive" is dominating the scene with the thought of a multi-national socialistic ruling body replacing the authority and responsibility that was and is the predestined mission of this nation. If that movement were to prove successful the American Race would no longer exist.

Jesus came into the world to do the will of His Father—all people are to be brought into eternal life through His work. In absolute dedication, without hesitation or doubt He followed the directive of His Father and is our greatest example of true leadership. His vision was focused on the mission, never wavering from the appointed task to do the will of The Father.

XII

THE CONCEPT OF SERVICE—
FINDING THE MIND OF A LEADER

Leadership implies the necessity of assistance required to accomplish a given task. With-in leadership there is work to be completed that cannot be done by one person. The leader must understand the reason, or purpose, for the mission and be able to convey that knowledge to those who are willing to follow, and in a manner that is acceptable to them.

The leader takes on the responsibility of the welfare of the team. The team needs to know what is expected of them but the leader must understand the capabilities and the limitations of each member. Helping them to become a vital part of the mission is not a simple task Competence and integrity are vital character traits that the leader must be able to discern in each of the team members.

We all need someone to follow, someone worthy of our trust. We expect to see a leader who is confident, observant, analytical, caring, praising—a role model, someone living a full life, someone whose influence is to be trusted—seen as authentic.

True leadership flows thru time spent in following, and learning—quickly, fluently, thoroughly—with an attitude that this is the best job in the world, demonstrating passion, desire, commitment, and dedication to the work and to his fellow worker, as well as to life.

Are you O.K. with this? Why?

Your personal sphere of influence is found within service to persons.

When a stone is dropped into the water the after effect, or influence of the fall, is seen in many ripples. The first action seen is the rising of the water in the center where the stone entered—this represents the self. The first ripple, or wave, represents our family—those to whom we are closest—those most affected by the action. That second ripple is our friends, persons whom we trust and who trust us. The third is our acquaintances, the persons that we nod to or with whom we have incidental relationships. The fourth represents strangers, the multitude of persons with whom we will never have a relationship. The ripples continue, affecting individuals we cannot perceive as even having lived. Like the stone passing through the water our action affects all of humanity.

Finally, there is no ripple remaining—nothing, no one is there to see or to know of our presence.

This stillness, silence, the time spent alone where no one sees—those secret places where we all go. It is in this time and area we are most able to determine what effect future personal activity will have on humanity, what influence will become manifest. What we pray, if we pray, what we read and watch, our thoughts and actions, the plans we form—all those activities that no one else will see or ever know about.—Secrets kept secret.

Not one ripple, it is here where the stone of tomorrow is formed, where the action that will be seen tomorrow is given birth. Here the heart is formed, here—character developed and future service determined.

The influence of service also is seen and felt in a logical connection to all humanity. The implication of servant to service is also logical. Service, like the falling stone, must be given mature and thoughtful consideration before it is released. In leadership the servant is seen as the one given completely to the mission as well as to the others who serve the same call. True leadership is service driven and is seen as such by those around it.

True leadership cannot be taken lightly; it is like a difficult dance—to be performed beautifully it requires training, practice and. time. There is an invisible box that each performer stands in. Each box or frame must be placed together with another, the basic steps memorized, synchronized and intimate. The important part of the dancer is hidden in the frame and needs to be revealed in the dance.

XIII

TO BELONG

Those qualities peculiar to a leader are also hidden—held in the "frame". The intimacy in leadership exposes the important qualities hidden in other persons allowing them to become that for which they were intended. Intimacy in men is found by encouraging them to tell their stories and listening to them, finding meaning, purpose and fulfillment within the group. The new person as well as the old person, all of us, want to be on the "inside" too, grateful to share life with someone, everyone. "To belong,—and to serve." and to be known, intimately—to be loved, and to love. This is the core of leadership.

We witness the truth in each persons need to be wanted in the recent protests around our nation and on "Wall Street". People, not sure of why they were there but knowing something in their homeland is not right, expressing their frustration and resentment in their sense of, or feeling of being passed over—left out of their share of life. Lost identities, not being needed, nor wanted, anticipating a meaningless and desperate tomorrow, they came looking for answers not found. Most of them were children of those whom we have named "Baby Boomers". They grew up in an era of the "Vietnam protest" seen on television along with increased violence and character assassinations. They have witnessed as acceptable the destruction of their brothers and sisters before birth. They have seen the Law of their Creator desecrated, the Law that formed this nation being denied before her citizenry, denied in our teaching and removed from our court houses and places of business. They have no mooring or anchor; no foundation, they are "as sheep having no shepherd".

Born to Lead? Really? Who is your councilor? Who do you turn to when everything is beyond your grasp? Where is your anchor and shield?

When we accept the Son of God as our redeemer we are given the Holy Spirit as our Councilor, to lead us into all truth, into righteousness and into holiness in order to become one with our Christ and with the Father and with each other. Without that unity this nation can not progress in its appointed destiny. Each person, being created in His image, is still endowed with those attributes of self will, intellect and authority.

Where truth is denied, knowledge and understanding fail and intellect ceases to lead. They bear witness to the condition of "all men", being created equal, endowed by their creator with those certain unalienable rights and still we turn our backs on the one who gives us council and are held captive once again by the tyranny of self exaltation whether it be our own or that of another.

XIV

ROADBLOCKS TO UNITY

Following is a list of some of the major roadblocks that stand in the way of unity with our Creator and with each other and within our nation. They also destroy the effective work of leadership and relationships in all avenues of life. They reflect in our character, the very heart of the person, and of a nation.

1. Anger
2. Bitterness
3. Resentment
4. Jealousy
5. Adultery
6. Wrath
7. Swearing
8. Envy
9. Lying
10. Gossip
11. Murder
12. Hatred
13. Selfishness
14. Coveting
15. Laziness

16. Slothfulness
17. Malice
18. Conniving
19. Disrespect
20. Acts of treason
21. Negligence
22. Slander
23. Theft
24. Self aggrandizement.
25. etc. etc. etc.

This list is by no means exhaustive and you may have a couple favorites of your own that are not included here. However, I ask you to pick a couple that you prefer and apply them to that other guy, you know, the person that just passed you on the freeway.

He's driving about 22 miles per hour over the speed limit, and, having just slowed down yourself because you know in your heart that there is a Highway Patrolman about four cars ahead of you. He's going to get caught.

My question is this: Why are you all of a sudden driving at that reduced speed?

My guess, born out of experience, is that—all of a sudden—some particular rule or regulation came to mind and for some reason you felt compelled to obey it. "Thou shalt not speed."?

Do you suppose that the reason for your sudden obedience was the realization that obeying the rule could save your life, or at least prevent serious injury to your self or someone else? Or, was it because you were lucky enough to have seen the cop in time?

Well, anyway, the guy got pulled over and is getting what he deserved and you and everyone else on the road are now back to your normal speed.

Hey! Everyone else is doing it! It's O.K.—unless you get caught, right?

Now lets' get back to your favorite pick from the list above. For just one week, while you are driving, every time you see a speed limit sign glance at your odometer and compare the condition of your driving with the condition of your character that is implied by the word you have selected.

I have spent a considerable amount of time dealing with this exercise. I'm not going to reveal my secret passion to you, but I can tell you this; it's not easy to slow down—every one else is doing it, you know. Prayer helps a lot, especially when it includes confession. I figure I need one more week,—at least.

While we are still dealing with this list of our "favorite attributes" ("or road blocks to unity") would you please turn back to that list and look closely at item number 14—"coveting" or covetousness; this possibly should have been at the top of list, or better still in a category all by itself. Personally I believe this condition is the primer or catalyst that triggers all of the other acts listed. It is the theme of the tenth Law of our Creator and is the precursor to the need of the nine that precede it.

When those listed roadblocks to unity are applied to the character of leadership we will see where trust is betrayed, integrity ceases, and unity fails. In considering each of those malignancies there can be found the supporting force of a lie. Once aroused, the lie will not be denied. It asks the question, "Where is your truth, O noble leader of men?" and what is your answer?

XV

TRUTH AND THE LIE

What is truth, the truth that sets you free?
By whose standard is a lie more vital than truth?
Why do we continue to perpetuate a lie and deny truth?
The lie has contaminated our integrity. Honor and virtue have
been set aside.

We have accepted the lie as a norm in our thinking and in our
daily relationships. It has brought separation into friendships
and families. The lie has brought anger, hatred and death. It
has created division in our entire existence, destroyed our
joy and there is no happiness. For the sake of the lie we have
successfully constructed our own personal prison, where life
itself holds little hope.

Unalienable life, liberty and happiness have become alien to us
as though they have now become the lie; something to be cast
aside.

Truth is not our enemy; it is not something to be feared.
Embrace it, respect it. If our faces and our work are to once

again reflect joy, peace and contentment, if we are to redeem our loving personal relationships with each other, if we are to be released from the chains that bind us because of the lie, we must expose the lie, and refuse to live with it.

The lie will not go away with out resistance.
It has cleverly imbedded itself into our daily existence.
Acknowledge its existence. We know it exists because of our reaction to it.
We are not free and the father of all lies will fight to keep us that way.
Pray. Confess some responsibility for the lie and ask for forgiveness and restoration with our Creator and with each other. Speak truth, expect resistance.
Truth suffered and all alone He died upon a cross. Still He remains the TRUTH.

What is truth?
It is liberty. It is freedom. It is love. It is what we are to be doing.
Even though we are given cause to deny Truth - He still remains.

"-------and the lie?"
This lie of lust, perpetuated by covetousness, is just one illustration of the power found in each of those "roadblocks to unity". Its legacy may very well be the destruction of that which is now American.

XVI

"—FALSEWITTNESS—
A LEGASY OF THE LIE—"

Friday evening, March 30, 2012—a little child sits on the floor by the end of the couch. She is holding herself in a fetal position, frowning and with a continence of hate, fear, and disgust. Hitting her self on the head with her hand she mutters "what's wrong with me? What's wrong with me!" Earlier in the week she had expressed how being yelled at made her feel angry.

This Childs' Father and Mother are in the final stages of divorce. They first met in a bar. Seven months after this little child was born they decided to marry. So, in the early part of a summer's day in a beautiful park, they gathered with a small group of witnesses and pledged a solemn oath to love, honor, and cherish each other until death and thus they began the realization of every newly wed persons dream—wedded bliss, happy, healthy children, a cottage on the top of the hill, roses 'round the door, trust, honor, integrity, and a deep abiding love that lasts forever—so the dream began.

This story is true and very personal. It is draining all joy and contentment from life for everyone near to it, tearing at the very soul of each of them. It reaches into relationships with those persons with whom each of them comes into contact. It carries itself into the depths of humanity and affects all of humankind. It is like the pebble dropped into the still, pure water. A splash, a ripple?' no—many ripples! They continue all the way across the pond. The pebble lands at the bottom of the pond. It arouses the sediment and thus it adulterates the once pure, clear, clean water. Its contamination has fulfilled its task, the contamination of the lie.

There sits a beautiful child with a beautiful mind, now possessed by a questioning guilt, for which she has no responsibility. Those who are responsible reject it, blaming others and refusing to acknowledge responsibility, casting all their anger and frustration into the mind of defenseless innocence.

Because of my personal bitterness and contempt for this function in life it is difficult for me to continue this exposé. I do not want to diminish the significance of its affect on me personally and all of those whom I hold dear. However, I know this scene is not unique to me alone but has been, and is still being played out many times over in the lives of a countless number of families. It would be very difficult if not impossible to truly evaluate the effect this condition has had on all of humanity. The impenetrable roadblock to such an evaluation is found in the unwillingness of persons, who are victims of this lie, to own or to confess any personal responsibility for it. I heard a young woman explain her pain from divorce this way "I'm awake now, and I have learned to hate the dream."

XVII

RESONSIBILITY FOR THE LIE

To some extent we are all responsible for the lie. Therefore, we are all responsible for its demise. It is not the dream that is the lie. It is the lie of self seeking—of placing personal passion and lust before reason that is the problem. It is the result of a permissive, immoral society. That does not diminish my own personal responsibility to express the truth nor does it diminish the responsibility of those of you who are receiving this thought. We have permitted and encouraged an immoral and perverse society to prevail in our midst. This lie has acquired such authority that it is tearing apart and destroying the very foundation of our existence as American. It extends itself into all humanity—intent upon destroying truth.

The condition has been in existence from far into the history of human kind. Its strength is found in an immoral and irreligious people. The American ideal was built on a foundation whose basis was a society of religion and morality, pillars that gave significance and meaning to each life and a sense of belonging and being needed to each of her people. Those basic principles of a free and prosperous people have been and are continuing to be replaced by the seeking after self centered pleasure and self exaltation. We are so absorbed in personal desire and ambition that we have become blinded to these evils surrounding us. We seek importance and guidance for our lives from others who are as lost and misguided as we are. It is a now a story of the blind leading the blind, with each party thinking the other is the leader, eventually blaming them for their lost condition and refusing to acknowledge the truth.

In years past men of honor and integrity who were seen in the political arena condemned the thought of adultery and divorce, considering them to be destroyers of fundamental liberty and as an affront to rational behavior in leadership, the profound destroyers of the foundation of the American.

Truth?—Divorce is not the only lie that denies truth. Others were previously listed as those "roadblocks to unity" with our Creator and with each of us. Divorce seems to stand out because of its frequency and prevalence in our society—in both the public and religious arena. It speaks of our personal moral and religious condition. Because of the familiarity we have with it—the way we each can acknowledge its affect on unity within our personal community—by comparison it serves to better understand the affect of the other lies herein called "roadblocks to our unity".

In attempting to keep this Trieste out of the realm of the personal and to reflect more on the society that is American I have found my self being drawn more and more into the affair. I feel an abiding need to be included with those who have been deemed "the little people" or the "uninformable"—those of us who have confidence in the Rule of Law as established through our Constitution by our Creator. It keeps us in protection from those who desire to place their personal authority above our own and to reduce our personal significance to something not much greater than chattel. Their work is to destroy personal freedoms and enslave the will. Their work is to take into captivity our intellect and our authority. Their desire is for our submission to them to be absolute. Their method is in our access to the Rule of Law being eliminated and replaced with an international progressive theology where the intellect, will and authority of their superior despot will guide us in all areas of our lives. For their illiberal progressive theology to be implemented our current form of governance must first be denied.

XVIII

WHEN MORALITY AND RELIGION FAIL

The "liberalization" of morality and the encouragement of the mockery of religious ideals have been with us through more than four decades.

The legalization of the killing of the innocent with the Roe verses Wade determination in 1973 has propelled the destruction of the American family.

The progressive thought is advancing.

The Law that preserves us is being denied.

Our first amendment rights are eroding away and each one of the other amendments are under attach

This race of people who are AMERICAN is in peril.

Mature reason and rational response are being demanded of each of us. It has never been more in need than at this time simply because it is on our watch. We have been given authority, intellect and will to be exercised to bring justice and liberty to all mankind. The time to respond is now, others served this call in the past and others will serve it in the future. Today is our time—this is the moment for us to decide and to act. We are AMERICAN and we shall prevail.

Please read the following words; spend some time in deep contemplation of what these words mean—what they are saying to you, about you, for you personally.

By your own reasoning—your intellect—what do they mean?

*** Amendment I

> Congress shall make no law respecting an establishment of religion, or prohibiting the free exercise thereof; or abridging the freedom of speech, or of the press; or the right of the people peaceably to assemble, and to petition the Government for a redress of grievances

*** Bill of Rights, 4 March, 1789, Congress of the United States.

Will the annulment of this law have any affect upon your will and your authority? Consider the affect it will have on your intellect, with a censored press where information is limited by a single controlling authority.

When our Creator said "Let us make man in our image" you were included, having been given authority, free will and an intellect. In History, whenever man has surrendered his morality and neglected his religious need he has always become the subject of the despot; authority is denied, the will suppressed, and information—knowledge—is transitive, perverting the intellect.

Are you willing to surrender your right to express your personal view? Today in this nation you can be prosecuted for speaking certain words that are considered to be not "politically correct". And what of your right to seek out and join with others in the "redress of grievances"?

At the beginning of the current war in Afghanistan we watched on television as a young woman with her head covered and dressed in blue was forced to kneel at the end of a soccer field. The next moment we saw her body suddenly lurch forward and lay lifelessly on the ground.

This past week I watched on television as a group of protestors now contained, hands tied, kneeling on the pavement while a uniformed police officer walked back and forth with a canister of pepper spray, spraying this group in their faces and on their heads over and over again. I wondered if it would have made any difference to him if he were carrying a loaded pistol instead of the canister. Why did the entire group of protesters just sit there and take it? The greater question is why didn't the other police officers intervene and stop their fellow comrade? Could this happen in the good old U.S. of A.? Or, has it already taken place? In Oakland?

Recently we have witnessed in several countries across the globe the rebellion of a people seeking freedom and liberty from the despot ruling over them. Their nations' military has been directed to annihilate their uprising. A nation has turned upon her citizenry, brothers and sisters, now in military uniform destroying their family homes, killing their civilian brothers and sisters, as well as their own mothers and fathers, relatives and friends, to preserve the hand of evil.

Do you believe this could happen on our homeland—in *** "the land of the free and the home of the brave"?

(*** A line of the lyrics from "Defense of Fort McHenry", a poem written in 1814 by the 35-year-old lawyer and amateur poet, Frances Scott Key, after witnessing the bombardment of Fort McHenry by the British Royal Navy ships in Chesapeake Bay during the Battle of Forte McHenry in the War of 1812.)

In all my being I pray that you can delve deeply into this question. Consider it for your personal liberties as well as for your family and children and for the future of this God given ideal that is American. Consider it for the mission for which this nation was called into existence to complete.

BALLETS OR BULLETS.—You can sit down and wait, or you can respond now. Your will is still your own. In waiting the inevitable will occur; despotism will be your destiny and eventually you will be forced to fight the battle over again.

That battle that has already been fought and has given to you the freedom that you now enjoy, will, out of the human condition, need to be fought once again, if you decide to wait.

Or,—you can wake up, acknowledge this responsibility, and understand this problem that is before us on this day, our day—study it, learn of it, and in your contemplation and decision use your authority as American to speak out, publish your rational thought, join in the voice of the assembly—and acknowledge your moral responsibility and vote, and bring your family and others whom you love to the voting booth with you. The excuse "maybe tomorrow" is no longer valid.

You choose. You decide—ballets today or bullets tomorrow. Personally I am praying for an informed electorate inclusive of you and those whom you love.

THE DECISION

God, bless us and bless this, our nation. Give us the will to keep and maintain that which you have so graciously given to us. Forgive us for our neglect of your call. Thank you for bestowing upon me the name "American".

Amen.

CONCLUSION

It well may be that the era of the American is finished, not by Gods' hand but by our own selfish neglect. It could be true that the "change" we were promised is complete and we are no longer a people of freedom and liberty but one given over to the rule of the despot. If so it is also the end of the American system of justice, of provision being made for the elderly, the poor and the helpless, for the widow and orphan. We may be, even now, reduced to the begging for mercy and alms where no one is there to hear. Unlimited governmental control perhaps has already replaced morality and religion in this nation.

Our moral compass is in need of repair. Religion is seen as archaic and repressive. No democratic nation can long exist in such a state of irreligion and immorality. The Law that was given to protect and to preserve us must once again be written on the hearts of our citizenry. It must be seen in our classrooms and in the public arena. Those values so vital to the men who founded this nation, pledging their lives, their fortunes and their sacred honor to preserve, must be re-instilled into the lives of our citizenry. The church must awaken and take back the territory it so thoughtlessly abandoned. It must speak out from the hilltops and from the public square. It can and must destroy this Goliath that seeks to enslave us, for its Word is all powerful and must be administered through the hand of righteousness, the authority that still remains with His Church.

AMERICAN, I plead with you; God gave this land to us for His good purpose. Let us preserve it with the certainty that we are "the nation of all nations"*** destined to be His vessel through which the salvation of all mankind is known.

Vote, vote in this national election.
Pray, pray for His protection on this American Race of His people.

Work, work to bring this message to every one you care about.

And let graciousness and attractiveness be known in your speech and in your work.

This is—AMERICAN—Gods servant to a lost world,—"a love story"

***"The Great Nation of Futurity," John L. O'Sullivan, 1839

—"I had a dream"—

TEXT SUMMMARY

Mr. Padelford sets forth the belief that being AMERICAN is a gift from our Creator God and a servant to a world of searching, lost and lonely humanity whose greatest need is to be intimately understood and to know they are loved. AMERICAN has no identifying qualities relative to race, gender, class or intellect but our commonality is found in our existence as being the creation of a loving God

His many years of service in the secular world and the Christian community have formed the conclusive thought contained in this brief writing. The philosophy and ideals that exist within political thought—whether it be democrat, republican, conservative, liberal or independent will make very little difference in the future of The United States of America without its return to the ideals that gave birth to this nation—principles founded in the Ten Commandments and precepts from our Holy Scripture.

He further believes regaining those principles and precepts will not be done without great sacrifice and hard work. Our nation has been straying away from her destiny for more than three generations.

The commitment must be total; not only within the political realm and national effort but more significantly in the hearts and minds of her people—individually, with each one of us actively pursuing our personal responsibility. Mature, sacrificial leadership must once again prevail.

The "liberalization" of morality and the encouragement of the mockery of religious ideals has been with us through more than four decades.

The legalization of the killing of the innocent with the Roe verses Wade determination in 1973 has propelled the destruction of the American family.

The Progressive Thought is advancing.

The Law that preserves us is being denied.

Our first amendment rights are eroding away and each one of the other amendments are under attach

This race of people who are AMERICAN is in peril

"The Church must reclaim her rightful place in the governance of persons".

BIBLIOGRAPHY AND RECOMMENDED READING

Holy Bible, NIV. Zondervan Publishing House. 1995

Robison, James. The Absolutes. Tyndale House, 2002.

Tournier, Paul. The Meaning of Persons. Harper and Row, Publishers. 1957

Dungy, Tony. The Mentor Leader. Tyndale House Publishers, 2010

Editors Robert Solomon and Mark Murphy, **What is Justice?** Oxford University Press, 1990.

O'toole, James. Creating The Good Life. Rodale, 2005.

REV Magazine, Interdenominational magazine for Pastors. Group Publishing, Inc.

Carnigie, Dale. Public Speaking and Influencing Men in Business, Association Press, 1955.

Overstreet, H.A. The Mature Mind, W. W. Norton and Company, Inc. 1949

The New Jerusalem Bible. Doubleday and Company, Inc. 1985.

The Liberty Collection. The Liberty Collection Group.

MacDonald, Gordon. Leadership (Journal for Church Leaders). 2005

www.ingramcontent.com/pod-product-compliance
Lightning Source LLC
Chambersburg PA
CBHW020357290526
45785CB00005B/2325